MW01173239

THE TEA LOVER'S Journal

Penelope Carlevato

Tea Lover's Journal
Copyright © 2019 Penelope M. Carlevato

All Rights Reserved. No part of this book may be reproduced, scanned or transmitted in any forms, digital, audio or printed without the expressed written consent of the author.

The information contained in this book are the views of the author based on her experiences and opinions.

Although the author and publisher have made every effort to ensure the information in this book was correct at press time, the author and publisher do not assume and hereby disclaim any liability to any party for any loss damage or disruption caused by errors or omissions, whether such errors or omissions result from negligence, accident or any other cause.

Introduction

Taking tea was often the way many women socialized, celebrated their friendships, and spent quiet, uninterrupted moments alone. From the Victorian era to the present, we savor this time-honored tradition of sharing our lives over a cup of tea.

I have always loved tea. I was born in a little village not far from Oxford, England, where tea was part of our daily life. My mother loved to have neighbors, family, and friends in for tea, and I always managed to find a place at the tea-table.

As I speak to women coast-to-coast, I find the love for the "quiet delight" of afternoon tea is a shared experience. The clink of bone china teacups, antique linens, and the gathering of friends is an activity loved by many. Whether it's tea in a mug at your kitchen table, in posh hotels in London, New York or Los Angeles, sinking into over-stuffed settees in English Country Manors, or seated in quaint little tearooms in the English countryside, a cup of tea is a welcome sight. I prefer to have tea at home, and I hope your home will be a favorite place for you, too!

Writing journal entries and taking tea go hand in hand. We are encouraged by those in the past who took the time to record their thoughts in their poems, stories, sonnets, and spiritual revelations.

Teatime is one of the fastest-growing trends in America. With that trend, a desire to slow down and enjoy life at a slower pace emerges. Journaling compliments teatime. As a cup of tea cannot be hurried, neither can our time spent writing our thoughts and insights. Recording events as they occur allows us to treasure the times at a later date.

The Bible tells us in the book of Proverbs (9:9 and 10:14) that wise men (and women) not only want to acquire knowledge for themselves but diligently seek more about ourselves and the world around us. Our personal goals and priorities need a place of accountability. What better avenue then daily journaling?

Journaling has no rules! It is entirely a voluntary discipline. Your way is the best for you, and your way is whatever you decide. This journal is purposely not dated so what and when you write is entirely up to you. Included are ideas and recipes to host your private tea time or tea parties.

I wish you blessings as you relax, pour yourself a cup of tea, and write your story. I will be thinking of you and know that you will find, as I did, slowing down and closing our mouth, opens our "ears" to hear!

Blessings in a teacup,

Other Books by Penelope M. Carlevato

Tea on the Titanic
First-Class Etiquette
The Art of Afternoon Tea: From the Era of Downton Abbey
and the Titanic.

*You can never get a cup of tea large enough or a
book long enough to suit me.*
C.S. Lewis

_____

_____

_____

_____

_____

_____

_____

_____

_____

_____

_____

_____

_____

_____

_____

_____

_____

_____

_____

_____

_____

_____

Tea to the English is really a picnic indoors.
Alice Walker

For my birthday, which is on the 4th of July, I had a most memorable tea with my daughters at the Savoy Hotel in London, England. The only thing missing was the fireworks!
Nanette Kinkade

_____

_____

_____

_____

_____

_____

_____

_____

_____

_____

_____

_____

_____

_____

_____

_____

_____

_____

_____

One of the charms of tea is the fact of drinking it together.
Edith Wharton

_____

_____

_____

_____

_____

_____

_____

_____

_____

_____

_____

_____

_____

_____

_____

_____

_____

_____

_____

_____

_____

_____

A woman is like a teabag - you can't tell how strong
she is until you put her in hot water.
Nancy Reagan

Offer hospitality to one another without grumbling.
I Peter 4:9

There is no trouble so great or grave that cannot be much diminished by a nice cup of tea.
Bernard-Paul Heroux

_____

_____

_____

_____

_____

_____

_____

_____

_____

_____

_____

_____

_____

_____

_____

_____

_____

_____

_____

_____

_____

Seize the moment. Remember all those women on the Titanic who waved off the dessert cart.
Erma Bombeck

I am a daughter of adventure. This means I never experience a dull moment and must be prepared for any eventuality.
Margaret (Molly) Brown

_____

_____

_____

_____

_____

_____

_____

_____

_____

_____

_____

_____

_____

_____

_____

_____

_____

_____

_____

_____

_____

_____

_____

Polly put the kettle on, we'll all have tea.
Charles Dickens

_____

_____

_____

_____

_____

_____

_____

_____

_____

_____

_____

_____

_____

_____

_____

_____

_____

_____

Tea drinking is above all a comforting ritual,
simultaneously soothing and stimulating, in which to withdraw
momentarily from the busyness of our lives.
Alexandra Stoddard

Thank God for tea! What would the world do without tea?
How did it exist? Am glad I was not born before tea!
Reverend Sydney Smith (1771-1845)

_____

_____

_____

_____

_____

_____

_____

_____

_____

_____

_____

_____

_____

_____

_____

_____

_____

_____

_____

_____

_____

_____

Early morning, noon or night, a cup of tea is my delight.

_____

_____

_____

_____

_____

_____

_____

_____

_____

_____

_____

_____

_____

_____

_____

_____

_____

_____

_____

_____

_____

_____

I believe it is customary in good society to take
some slight refreshment at five o'clock.
Oscar Wilde

_____

_____

_____

_____

_____

_____

_____

_____

_____

_____

_____

_____

_____

_____

_____

_____

_____

_____

_____

There is much of mystery, poetry, and romance in the march of tea down through the years.
William Ukers

There are few hours in life more agreeable than the hour
dedicated to the ceremony known as afternoon tea.
Henry James

_____

_____

_____

_____

_____

_____

_____

_____

_____

_____

_____

_____

_____

_____

_____

_____

_____

_____

_____

_____

_____

If a stranger says unto thee that he thirsted,
give him a cup of tea.
Confucius

_____

_____

_____

_____

_____

_____

_____

_____

_____

_____

_____

_____

_____

_____

_____

_____

_____

_____

_____

_____

Taste and see that the Lord is good.
Psalm 34:8

_____

_____

_____

_____

_____

_____

_____

_____

_____

_____

_____

_____

_____

_____

_____

_____

_____

_____

_____

_____

_____

Tea cleared my head and left me with no misapprehensions.
Duke of Wellington

In nothing more is the English genius for domesticity more
notably declared than in the institution of this festival –
almost one may call it - of afternoon tea.
The mere clink of cups and saucers tunes the mind to happy repose.
George Gissing

_____

_____

_____

_____

_____

_____

_____

_____

_____

_____

_____

_____

_____

_____

_____

_____

_____

_____

_____

_____

_____

But indeed, I would rather have nothing but tea.
Jane Austen

_____

_____

_____

_____

_____

_____

_____

_____

_____

_____

_____

_____

_____

_____

_____

_____

_____

_____

_____

_____

It's a very good English custom, though the weather is
cold or hot when you need a little pick-up, you'll find
a little teacup will always hit the spot.
Jack Buchanan

_____

_____

_____

_____

_____

_____

_____

_____

_____

_____

_____

_____

_____

_____

_____

_____

_____

_____

_____

_____

Tea gives vigor of body, the contentment of mind, and determination of purpose when taken over a long period of time.
Lu Yu

_____

_____

_____

_____

_____

_____

_____

_____

_____

_____

_____

_____

_____

_____

_____

_____

_____

_____

_____

_____

Love and scandal are the best sweeteners of tea.
Henry Fielding

Stands the church clock at ten to three?
And is there honey still for tea?
Rupert Brook

_____

_____

_____

_____

_____

_____

_____

_____

_____

_____

_____

_____

_____

_____

_____

_____

_____

_____

_____

_____

_____

_____

_____

*My dear, if you could give me a cup of tea to clear my muddle of a
head I should better understand your affairs.*
Charles Dickens (1812-1870)

_____

_____

_____

_____

_____

_____

_____

_____

_____

_____

_____

_____

_____

_____

_____

_____

_____

_____

_____

To beat fatigue you'll all agree, there's nothing like a cup of tea!

A friend loves at all times.
Proverbs 17:17

_____

_____

_____

_____

_____

_____

_____

_____

_____

_____

_____

_____

_____

_____

_____

_____

_____

_____

_____

_____

_____

_____

_____

_____

_____

Better to be deprived of food for three days, than tea for one.
Ancient Chinese Proverb

_____

_____

_____

_____

_____

_____

_____

_____

_____

_____

_____

_____

_____

_____

_____

_____

_____

_____

_____

_____

_____

_____

_____

_____

Each cup of tea represents an imaginary voyage.
Catherine Douzel

_____

_____

_____

_____

_____

_____

_____

_____

_____

_____

_____

_____

_____

_____

_____

_____

_____

_____

_____

_____

_____

_____

_____

Cynthia came in quietly and set a cup of tea before him. He kissed her hand, inexpressibly grateful, and she went back into the kitchen. When we view the little things with thanksgiving, even they become big things.
Jan Karon, *These High, Green Hills*

_____

_____

_____

_____

_____

_____

_____

_____

_____

_____

_____

_____

_____

_____

_____

_____

_____

_____

_____

(I am) a hardened and shameless tea-drinker, who has for twenty years diluted his meals with only the infusion of this fascinating plant; whose kettle has scarcely time to cool; who with tea amuses the evening, with tea solaces the midnight, and with tea welcomes the morning.
Dr. Samuel Johnson (1709 - 1784)

_____

_____

_____

_____

_____

_____

_____

_____

_____

_____

_____

_____

_____

_____

_____

_____

_____

_____

_____

_____

_____

I love to mix teas. My favorite blend of tea is
half Earl Grey and half Lapsong Suchong.
Sarah, The Duchess of York

The hot water is to remain upon the tea leaves no longer than you
can say the Miserere (Psalm 51) very leisurely.
Sir Kenelm Digby (1603-1665)

_____

_____

_____

_____

_____

_____

_____

_____

_____

_____

_____

_____

_____

_____

_____

_____

_____

_____

_____

_____

_____

_____

There are few more agreeable moments in life than tea in an English country house in winter.
William Lyon Phelps

_____

_____

_____

_____

_____

_____

_____

_____

_____

_____

_____

_____

_____

_____

_____

_____

_____

_____

_____

_____

_____

_____

Afternoon tea - that pleasant hour
When children are from lessons free,
And gather round their social board
Brimful of mirth and childish glee.
J. C. Sowerby and H. H. Emmerson

_____

_____

_____

_____

_____

_____

_____

_____

_____

_____

_____

_____

_____

_____

_____

_____

_____

_____

_____

_____

_____

_____

We can survive functional illiteracy or shattered windows of vulnerability, but not the demise of the decent cup of tea.
Malachi McCormick

_____

_____

_____

_____

_____

_____

_____

_____

_____

_____

_____

_____

_____

_____

_____

_____

_____

_____

_____

_____

_____

_____

_____

_____

The gardens at Buckingham Palace - Tea is served, the National Anthem is played, and the Queen comes out into the garden with members of the Royal Family to walk among her guests.
Sheila Pickles, *The Essence of English Life*

Accept life daily not as a cup to be drained, but as a
chalice to be filled with whatsoever things are
honest, pure, lovely and of good report.
Sidney Lovett

_____

_____

_____

_____

_____

_____

_____

_____

_____

_____

_____

_____

_____

_____

_____

_____

_____

_____

_____

_____

Thanks for the kind thoughts. Water was fine and swimming good.
Neptune was exceedingly kind to me and I am now high and dry.
Margaret (Molly) Brown (after her experience on the Titanic.)

_____

_____

_____

_____

_____

_____

_____

_____

_____

_____

_____

_____

_____

_____

_____

_____

_____

_____

_____

Stay is a charming word in a friend's vocabulary.
Louisa May Alcott

_____

_____

_____

_____

_____

_____

_____

_____

_____

_____

_____

_____

_____

_____

_____

_____

_____

_____

_____

_____

_____

Sunday afternoon is special to us. This is the time when we sit down to a proper tea. You can always count on Sunday teatime at our house, with a vast pot of tea.
Elizabeth Brooks

Tea in the cup first. I never take sugar in tea.
Julian Fellows

_____

_____

_____

_____

_____

_____

_____

_____

_____

_____

_____

_____

_____

_____

_____

_____

_____

_____

_____

A cup of tea, a prayer or two, blessed moments,
shared with you.
Ellen Cuomo

_____

_____

_____

_____

_____

_____

_____

_____

_____

_____

_____

_____

_____

_____

_____

_____

_____

_____

_____

_____

_____

_____

_____

Tea is the ultimate form of hospitality.
Amy Vanderbilt

_____

_____

_____

_____

_____

_____

_____

_____

_____

_____

_____

_____

_____

_____

_____

_____

_____

_____

_____

_____

_____

_____

When the tea is brought at five o'clock,
And all the curtains are drawn with care,
The little black cat with bright green eyes
Is suddenly purring there.
Harold Monro

_____

_____

_____

_____

_____

_____

_____

_____

_____

_____

_____

_____

_____

_____

_____

_____

_____

_____

_____

_____

People all over the world take their time in making tea,
as if to acknowledge that making it is part of drinking
it and drinking it represents a refuge, a moment's
respite, from the demands of our lives.
James Norwood Pratt

_____

_____

_____

_____

_____

_____

_____

_____

_____

_____

_____

_____

_____

_____

_____

_____

_____

_____

She found a cloth and laid the tea, setting out cakes and biscuits,
sugar bowl and silver milk jug.
Even for kitchen tea, it appeared, her standards were meticulous.
Rosamunde Pilcher, *The Day of the Storm*

_____

_____

_____

_____

_____

_____

_____

_____

_____

_____

_____

_____

_____

_____

_____

_____

_____

_____

_____

_____

Whether a grand celebration or a humble meeting of two friends at the kitchen table, tea with a little something remains an important part of English daily life.
Catherine Calvert, *The Heart of England*

I select my tea rather as I select my perfume - to match my mood
and the season.
Sheila Pickles, *The Essence of English Life*

_____

_____

_____

_____

_____

_____

_____

_____

_____

_____

_____

_____

_____

_____

_____

_____

_____

_____

_____

_____

_____

When the days are short and night draws in at teatime, English family life centers around the fire.
Sheila Pickles, *The Essence of English Life*

---

*The "Royals" (Royal Family) always see people they don't much
want to see for tea. They can get away quickly,
but they have been polite and called.*
Stephen P. Barry Royal Service

_____

_____

_____

_____

_____

_____

_____

_____

_____

_____

_____

_____

_____

_____

_____

_____

_____

_____

_____

_____

_____

_____

They're changing guard at Buckingham Palace-
Christopher Robin went down with Alice.
Do you think the King knows all about me?
Sure to, dear, but it's time for tea.
A.A. Milne

In my darkest days, tea with the children was one of the highlights of the day, as I relished the thought of all those comforts laid out before me. Tea is still important to us.
Sarah, The Duchess of York

_____

_____

_____

_____

_____

_____

_____

_____

_____

_____

_____

_____

_____

_____

_____

_____

_____

_____

_____

_____

_____

_____

Tea urges tranquility of the soul.
Henry Wadsworth Longfellow

_____

_____

_____

_____

_____

_____

_____

_____

_____

_____

_____

_____

_____

_____

_____

_____

_____

_____

_____

_____

_____

_____

Come and share a pot of tea, my home is warm
and my friendship's free.
Emilie Barnes

_____

_____

_____

_____

_____

_____

_____

_____

_____

_____

_____

_____

_____

_____

_____

_____

_____

_____

_____

_____

_____

As I pour my tea in the morning, I think of the aunts who gave us the tea service when we were married.
Sheila Pickles, *The Essence of English Life*

---

*For tea, though ridiculed by those who are naturally
coarse in their nervous sensibilities…will always be the favored
beverage of the intellectual.*
Thomas De Quincey (1785-1859)

_____

_____

_____

_____

_____

_____

_____

_____

_____

_____

_____

_____

_____

_____

_____

_____

_____

_____

_____

_____

Happy is the house that shelters a friend.
Ralph Waldo Emerson

It is important from time to time to slow down - to go away by yourself and simply be - and brew a cup of tea.
Eileen Caddy

_____

_____

_____

_____

_____

_____

_____

_____

_____

_____

_____

_____

_____

_____

_____

_____

_____

_____

_____

_____

_____

Whatever you do, in word or deed, do it all in the name of the Lord.
Colossians 3:17

_____

_____

_____

_____

_____

_____

_____

_____

_____

_____

_____

_____

_____

_____

_____

_____

_____

_____

_____

_____

_____

_____

Teaism is the discipline of the mind, body, heart, and spirit.
Okakura Kakuzo (1862-1913)

_____

_____

_____

_____

_____

_____

_____

_____

_____

_____

_____

_____

_____

_____

_____

_____

_____

_____

_____

_____

_____

_____

_____

If you are cold, tea will warm you-
If you are heated, it will cool you-
If you are depressed, it will cheer you,
If you are excited, it will calm you.
William E. Gladstone

_____

_____

_____

_____

_____

_____

_____

_____

_____

_____

_____

_____

_____

_____

_____

_____

_____

_____

_____

_____

Hospitality is a wonderful thing. It warms the heart and sharpens the wits by the interchange of ideas.
Tea and Conversation

Friends put the entire world to right over a cup of tea.
Charlotte Gray

_____

_____

_____

_____

_____

_____

_____

_____

_____

_____

_____

_____

_____

_____

_____

_____

_____

_____

_____

_____

_____

Enjoy life sip by sip, not gulp by gulp.
The Minister of Leaves

It is good to remember that the tea kettle, although up to its neck in hot water, continues to sing.

Afternoon tea should not be a filling meal.
It is meant to accompany a cup of tea. The main
purpose is to bridge the gap between lunch and
dinner and provide a venue for friendship.

_____
_____
_____
_____
_____
_____
_____
_____
_____
_____
_____
_____
_____
_____
_____
_____
_____
_____
_____
_____

We always have our afternoon tea, mind you.
If you don't keep the inner man going, you can't
keep the outer one going, can you?
Winifred Westcott

_____

_____

_____

_____

_____

_____

_____

_____

_____

_____

_____

_____

_____

_____

_____

_____

_____

_____

_____

_____

_____

Tea gives vigor of body, the contentment of mind,
and determination of purpose when taken
over a long period of time.
Lu Yu

Teach me the art of creating islands of stillness, in which
I can absorb the beauty of everyday things.
Marian Stroud

_____

_____

_____

_____

_____

_____

_____

_____

_____

_____

_____

_____

_____

_____

_____

_____

_____

_____

_____

_____

*Come, oh, come ye tea-thirsty restless ones-the
kettle boils, bubbles and sings musically.*

Great love affairs start with Champagne and end with tea.
Honore' de Balzac

_____
_____
_____
_____
_____
_____
_____
_____
_____
_____
_____
_____
_____
_____
_____
_____
_____
_____
_____
_____
_____
_____
_____
_____

There is a great deal of poetry and fine sentiment in a chest of tea.
Ralph Waldo Emerson

_____

_____

_____

_____

_____

_____

_____

_____

_____

_____

_____

_____

_____

_____

_____

_____

_____

_____

_____

_____

_____

_____

Tea, Heav'ns delight, and nature's truest wealth.
Peter Antoine Motteux

_____

_____

_____

_____

_____

_____

_____

_____

_____

_____

_____

_____

_____

_____

_____

_____

_____

_____

_____

_____

_____

_____

During the bombing in London in WW II, as soon as the
all clear sirens sounded, we left our bomb shelters and
immediately put the kettle on for tea.
Thelma Barrett Schwarting

_____

_____

_____

_____

_____

_____

_____

_____

_____

_____

_____

_____

_____

_____

_____

_____

_____

_____

_____

_____

_____

_____

_____

_____

Although my neighbors are all barbarians, and you, you are a thousand miles away; there are always two cups on my table.
Saying from the Tang Dynasty

_____

_____

_____

_____

_____

_____

_____

_____

_____

_____

_____

_____

_____

_____

_____

_____

_____

_____

_____

_____

_____

_____

On wings of hospitality, she flew to brew the tea.
Tom Hegg, *A Cup of Christmas Tea*

_____

_____

_____

_____

_____

_____

_____

_____

_____

_____

_____

_____

_____

_____

_____

_____

_____

_____

_____

_____

_____

_____

_____

_____

Sometimes teas will warm you, sometimes teas are cold
I see how tea is just like life, now that I am old.
Rose Sweet

_____

_____

_____

_____

_____

_____

_____

_____

_____

_____

_____

_____

_____

_____

_____

_____

_____

_____

_____

_____

_____

*Somehow, taking tea together encourages an atmosphere of
intimacy when you slip off the timepiece in your mind and cast
your fate to a delight of tasty tea, tiny foods,
and thoughtful conversation.*
Gail Greco

Afternoon tea can be anything from an intimate gathering around a roaring fire on a winter afternoon to a relaxed party in the garden on a sunny summer day.
Lesley Mackley

_____

_____

_____

_____

_____

_____

_____

_____

_____

_____

_____

_____

_____

_____

_____

_____

_____

_____

_____

_____

_____

A tearoom is a most relaxing spot, with decadent pampering
I like a lot; but sometimes I just want to be alone,
with my journal, tea, and a scone.

*We'll have a tea said she, a birthday tea for me? Oh yes, it will be
quite divine, as you sip yours and I sip mine!*
Dolley Carlson

_____

_____

_____

_____

_____

_____

_____

_____

_____

_____

_____

_____

_____

_____

_____

_____

_____

_____

_____

_____

There is nothing like staying at home for real comfort.
Jane Austen

_____

_____

_____

_____

_____

_____

_____

_____

_____

_____

_____

_____

_____

_____

_____

_____

_____

_____

_____

_____

_____

_____

_____

"You won't learn this in textbooks," she said softly to me-
"how you can lift another's soul with just a cup of tea."
Carla Muir

_____

_____

_____

_____

_____

_____

_____

_____

_____

_____

_____

_____

_____

_____

_____

_____

_____

_____

_____

_____

*She was a fine woman, a perfect gentlewoman. She had taken
life, as she liked a cup of tea - weak, with an exquisite
aroma and plenty of milk and sugar.*
Henry James

_____

_____

_____

_____

_____

_____

_____

_____

_____

_____

_____

_____

_____

_____

_____

_____

_____

_____

_____

_____

"Won't ye sit and have a cup of tea?" The deacon sat, and
when Mary passed him his cup, he looked down in surprise
and exclaimed: "Why, Mary! It's only water ye have!"
"Aye!" said old Mary. "But He makes it taste like tea!"
Ruth Bell Graham, *A Taste of Tea*

Tea is the drink of friendship.
Sarah Jane Evans and Giles Hilton

Some days can get you going, others calm you down
It's clear, My dear that life, like tea,
Tastes Sweeter in a Crown!
Rose Sweet

_____

_____

_____

_____

_____

_____

_____

_____

_____

_____

_____

_____

_____

_____

_____

_____

_____

_____

_____

_____

_____

The pleasures of afternoon tea run like a trickle of honey through English literature from Rupert Brook's wistful line on the Old Vicarage at Grantchester to Miss Marple, calmly dissecting a case over tea cakes at a seaside hotel.
Stan Hay

*Rainy days should be spent at home with
a cup of tea and a good book.*
Bill Watterson

Writing is a job, a talent, but it's also the place to go in your head.
It is the imaginary friend you drink your tea with in the afternoon.
Ann Patchett

_____

_____

_____

_____

_____

_____

_____

_____

_____

_____

_____

_____

_____

_____

_____

_____

_____

_____

_____

_____

_____

A great idea should always be left to steep like loose tea leaves in a teapot for awhile to make sure that the tea will be strong enough and the idea truly is a great one.
Phoebe Stone

This, then, is what tea means to me: the embrace of friendship,
quiet contemplation, and the sustenance that can
bring inner serenity and peace.
Dianna Rosen

_____

_____

_____

_____

_____

_____

_____

_____

_____

_____

_____

_____

_____

_____

_____

_____

_____

_____

_____

_____

_____

Where even the tea kettle sings from happiness. That is home.
Ernestine Schumann Heink

_____

_____

_____

_____

_____

_____

_____

_____

_____

_____

_____

_____

_____

_____

_____

_____

_____

_____

_____

_____

The cup of tea on arrival at a country house is a thing which, as a rule, I particularly enjoy. I like the crackling logs, the shaded lights, the scent of buttered toast, the general atmosphere of leisured coziness.
P.G Wodehouse

I smile, of course, and go on drinking tea, yet with these April sunsets, that somehow recall my buried life, and Paris in the Spring. I feel immeasurably at peace, and find the world to be wonderful and youthful, after all.
T.S. Eliot

In a crisis we English often say, "Come on, sit down and have a cup of tea and we'll talk about it. I can't tell you how often in my life I've heard those words.
Rose Tanner

_____

_____

_____

_____

_____

_____

_____

_____

_____

_____

_____

_____

_____

_____

_____

_____

_____

_____

_____

_____

_____

_____

Tea urges tranquility of the soul.
William Wordsworth Longfellow

Our children know, whatever happen, at five I am invariably home for tea. They all think of tea rather like I do really. It's a tradition they would hate to be broken.
Virginia, Lady Bath, Marchioness of Bath

_____

_____

_____

_____

_____

_____

_____

_____

_____

_____

_____

_____

_____

_____

_____

_____

_____

_____

_____

_____

*Sunday afternoon is special to us. This is the time when
we sit down to a proper tea. It's a lovely way for us
all to be together at teatime.*
Elizabeth Brooks

_____

_____

_____

_____

_____

_____

_____

_____

_____

_____

_____

_____

_____

_____

_____

_____

_____

_____

_____

_____

_____

*Of tea…Its proper use is to amuse the idle, relax
the studious and dilute the full meals of those who
cannot use exercise and will not use abstinence.*
Samuel Johnson

Afternoon Tea should be provided, fresh supplies, with thin bread-and-butter, fancy pastries, cakes, etc., being brought in as other guests arrive.
Mrs. Beeton, *The Book of Household Management*

_____

_____

_____

_____

_____

_____

_____

_____

_____

_____

_____

_____

_____

_____

_____

_____

_____

_____

_____

_____

_____

_____

If life is a cup of tea, gratitude is the honey that makes it sweet.
Natasha Potter.

My Great Grandmother, Margaret (Molly) Brown, loved raspberries and cream for breakfast with her morning cup of tea.
Helen Benziger

Offer hospitality to one another without grumbling.
I Peter 4:9

_____

_____

_____

_____

_____

_____

_____

_____

_____

_____

_____

_____

_____

_____

_____

_____

_____

_____

_____

_____

_____

_____

Types of Teas

A. Afternoon Tea: A delightful event usually at 4
    o'clock. There are three courses and served in this
    order: savories, scones and lastly, sweets or
    pastries.

B. Cream Tea: Also served at 4 o'clock, consists of a
    pot of tea and scones with clotted cream and jam.

C. High Tea: An early evening meal or supper (5 or 6
    o'clock) consisting of a hot meat or cheese dish,
    bread, cakes and tea. High tea is not to be
    confused with the more elegant Afternoon Tea.

Making a Proper Cup of Tea

- Pour fresh cold water into the kettle.
- Warm the teapot with hot tap water.
- When water comes to a boil, pour out water from the teapot
- Spoon tea into the teapot.
- Measure tea according to the size of the teapot. A small teapot usually serves 2; a medium teapot serves 4 and a large teapot serves 6. A good rule of thumb is one teaspoon for every two cups of tea. If using tea bags, one teabag for every two cups.
- Pour the boiling water into the teapot, over the tea leaves and let brew for three to five minutes. Use a tea cozy if desired.
- Pour the tea into the teacups using a strainer.
- The new infuser baskets are a great way to make tea. Just remove the basket when the tea is finished brewing.

Making Iced Tea

Follow the steps for making hot tea, but use more tea, almost twice as much. Do not refrigerate until the tea has come to room temperature. Pour over ice cubes and enjoy. A few springs of mint adds a delightful taste. Allow each guest to add sugar if desired.

Decaffeinated Tea

Start by preparing tea the proper way, but just cover the tea leaves with about an inch of water. Brew for 30 to 45 seconds, and then pour off the water. Pour boiling water back over the tea leaves and brew as directed for 3-5 minutes. You will have removed most of the caffeine, but still, have wonderful tea.

Storing Tea

Keep tea in a tightly covered ceramic or tin container. Keep away from sunlight and heat. Do not refrigerate or freeze. Tea will stay fresh for up to 18 to 24 months if stored properly.

Tea Etiquette

- The hostess pours the tea and then passes the responsibility to her best friend.
- The teacup and saucer should be left on the table before pouring the tea rather than someone holding the cup.
- Milk and sugar cubes are put into the cup before the tea.
- Quietly stir your tea with your teaspoon
- No crooking of pinkie finger when drinking tea.
- Do not fill the teacup to the rim.
- Remove gloves when eating and drinking tea.
- Cut scone in half, and then apply jam first, then the cream. Do not put the scone back together but eat open-faced.
- Assign seats if having a sit-down tea.
- Keep purses, keys, and glasses off the tea table.
- Serve the three tea courses in order: sandwiches, scones then desserts.
- If served a teabag, place the teabag into the teapot, not the cup.
- Do not squeeze the teabag after use or bounce it up and down to speed the brewing time.
- If drinking tea around a coffee table, always bring the saucer with the teacup.

Recipes
Sandwiches

Deviled Ham Sandwich

- 1 small can deviled ham
- 1/4 cup finely chopped green onion
- 1 Tab. Dijon Mustard

Combine all ingredients, spread on buttered slices of wheat bread. Trim crusts and cut into desired shapes.

Curried Chicken Tea Sandwich

- 2 cups cooked and chopped chicken breasts (or 1 large can of canned chicken, drained)
- 1/4 cup Mayonnaise
- 2 green onions (finely chopped)
- 1/4 cup chopped cashews
- 1/2 tsp. of curry powder.

Mix above together - spread on buttered bread, trim crusts and cut into desired shapes. Makes 20 tea sandwiches.

Cucumber Tea Sandwich

Wash and slice one English hothouse cucumber as thin as possible. Place in a colander and sprinkle with a little vinegar and salt. Put a plate on top of cucumbers to weight it down. Leave to drain for at least 30 minutes. Place cucumber on paper towels and press out any remaining liquid. Spread white bread with softened cream cheese and cover with cucumber slices sprinkle lightly with dill. Top with the second slice of buttered bread, trim crusts and cut into four fingers shaped sandwiches. *For a spicier taste, add 1 tsp. of horseradish to cream cheese.

Egg Salad Sandwiches

- 6 hard-boiled eggs, remove shells and soak in Earl Grey tea for several hours.
- 1/4 cup finely chopped green onion
- 1/4 cup sweet pickle relish
- 1/3 cup mayonnaise
- 1/2 tsp. salt
- 1/4 tsp. Pepper

Combine all ingredients well, chill, and then spread thinly on buttered slices of bread. Trim crusts and cut into desired shapes.

Tips for Sandwich Making

- Use thinly sliced or sandwich bread...a mix of wheat and white. Pullman loaves ordered from a bakery also work nicely. Make your own bread and add food coloring with the liquid, before the mixing. One sandwich loaf of bread will make about 40 tea sandwiches. (quarters)

- Make each kind of sandwich the same shape. Such as all the egg salad - squares, the chicken - triangles, the cucumber - fingers, etc.

- Freeze bread before making sandwiches.

- Seal bread with butter or cream cheese to prevent soggy sandwiches.

- Keep filling for sandwiches moderately applied, not too thick.

- Cut off the crusts and into shapes with an electric knife.

- After making sandwiches, place in a waxed paper-lined plastic container, cover with a damp paper towel or lettuce leaves, then plastic wrap before sealing. Keep refrigerated until use.

Scones

Penelope's Royal Scones

- 3 1/4 cups self-rising flour
- 1/3 cup sugar
- 1/2 cup butter, cut into small pieces
- 3/4 cup buttermilk (Substitute 3/4 cup milk with 2 tsp. lemon juice)

Mix flour & sugar together with a whisk. Cut butter into flour and sugar with a pastry blender until it resembles fine breadcrumbs. Make a well in the center of the mix and add buttermilk. Mix lightly with a fork until a soft dough is formed. Put onto a lightly floured surface and gently knead a few times. Roll or press dough out to 1" thick. Cut into 2 1/2-inch circles with biscuit cutter and place on lightly greased cookie sheet, spaced a little apart.

Gather trimmings and repeat until dough is all used. Brush tops with milk or beaten egg.

Bake at 375° F for 12 to 15 minutes, until just lightly brown on top. (Dried currants or dried fruit may be added after buttermilk). Mix 1/4-cup dried fruit with 2 tsp. flour and add to scone mixture.) Makes 12 scones. Serve with clotted cream and jam.

Mock Devonshire Cream or Clotted Cream

- 2 cups heavy whipping cream
- 1 to 2 drops of yellow food coloring

Add food coloring to whipping cream. Beat cream until very stiff. Store in refrigerator in a glass container until ready to use. Serve with warm scones.

"Real" Devonshire or Clotted Cream can be bought in the refrigerated section at specialty markets.

To properly eat scones with jam and cream, cut the scone in half like a hamburger bun. If you do it the way they do in Devon, you will put the cream on first then the jam. If you are in Cornwall, the jam goes on first, then the cream.

—OR—

You can break off a piece of the scone, place jam and cream on your plate, then put jam and cream on each bite. Enjoy!

Sweets

Shortbread Cookies

- 1 cup butter, softened
- 1/2 cup sugar
- 2 cups flour, sifted

  - Cream together butter and sugar, gradually work in flour with your hands until you have a smooth, binding consistency.

  - On a lightly floured surface, knead well to a smooth dough and roll out to 1/2 inch thick.

  - Cut the dough into fingers or use a cookie cutter.
  - Place on cookie sheet and prick the top of the cookies with a fork.

  - Bake at 350 for about 15 to 20 minutes, until very pale golden. Leave for 1 minute to cool, then transfer to a wire rack and sprinkle well with sugar while still warm.

  - Store in an airtight container, when cool. Don't overbake; cookies are done when pale golden, tops will feel dry.

Rachel's Victorian Sandwich Cake

- 1 cup butter, softened
- 1 cup sugar
- 3 eggs
- 2 cups self-rising flour
  *You may use a package of white cake mix and follow directions

- Lemon Curd or Raspberry or Strawberry Jam
- 2 cups whipping cream, whipped

1. Grease and line two 8-inch round cake tins with parchment paper.
2. Preheat oven to 350°F
3. Cream butter and sugar, add eggs and mix well.
4. Gradually add and fold in flour.
5. Bake 30 minutes at 350°F
6. Cool on rack, then remove from pans and put one-layer top side up on serving plate.
7. Sandwich bottoms of cake together with jam or lemon curd, and the whipped cream.
8. Sprinkle powdered sugar on top of cake, then decorate with fresh strawberries, raspberries or edible flowers.

Places where I love to have tea:

_____

_____

_____

_____

_____

_____

_____

_____

_____

_____

_____

_____

_____

_____

_____

_____

_____

_____

_____

_____

_____

_____

The Friendly Road

There's a beautiful road, a Friendly road
That runs through this little earth
Where heart meets heart in a pleasant way
That cheers with its warmth and mirth:
It's a road where the sky is fair and blue
When traveled with friends who are strong and true,
It's a beautiful road that stops for tea
While my friend and I meet in harmony.
Unknown

About the author

Penelope Carlevato — British born and raised in the US. She is an avid tea drinker and spent many years as a Registered Nurse. She was the founder and owner of the retail tea business, Penelope's Tea Time, for over two decades. She is an award-winning author, speaker and personality coach.

She is a speaker to women's groups, historical organizations, and business events. Penelope is a member of the Advanced Writers and Speakers Association, the Titanic Speakers Bureau, Christian Women Speakers and MOPS Speaker Network. She serves as a regular columnist for Leading Hearts, the award-winning magazine for Christian women, and also writes for the quarterly magazine, Innovative Health. As a Registered Nurse, she writes for medical, health, and wellness magazines.

Her three books are: *Tea on the Titanic, First Class Etiquette* and *The Art of Afternoon Tea.*

A love of the Edwardian era and the traditions of that period provide the motivation for her books. She resides in Colorado with her husband, Norman. They are the grandparents of 11 and great-grandparents of two.

To book Penelope for your group or event:
www.PenelopeCarlevato.com
PenelopesTeaTime@gmail.com

Made in the USA
Columbia, SC
19 June 2023

17968529R00081